Dedications

To all of you whose unique contributions make our world so colorful. Keep "painting"!
—Keith Thomas

~

To Romario, who changed my world, making it more beautiful and colorful. I love you.
—Melodee Strong

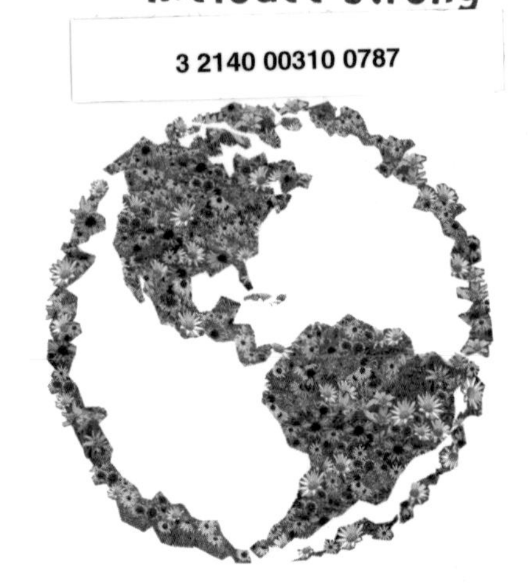

Ages 5 and up

Maren Green Publishing, Inc.
5525 Memorial Avenue North, Suite 6
Oak Park Heights, MN 55082
Toll-free 800-287-1512

Library of Congress Control Number: 2007907861

Edited by Pamela Espeland

Text set in Slappy Inline
Illustrations created using acrylic and collage on wood

First Edition December 2007
10 9 8 7 6 5 4 3 2 1
Manufactured in China

ISBN: 978-1-934277-13-3

www.marengreen.com

Colorful World

Includes a CD of the song "COLORFUL WORLD" by Six-time Grammy winner CECE WINANS

Lyrics by CeCe Winans, Keith Thomas, and Alvin Love III
Illustrated by Melodee Strong

Maren Green Publishing, Inc.
Oak Park Heights, Minnesota

She wears nose rings
with weird things

floating through her hair.

She is slightly
embarrassed
by everyone who stares.

And when she walks away,
you might say
she's a little wild.

But she could rule the world
when she opens up her mouth
and smiles.

It's a colorful world that we live in.
A beautiful world that we live in.

He's been cheated,
mistreated,
for the color of his skin.

APPLES
50¢ea.

He is rarely
contrary
over what should not
have been.

Yet he holds his head up
instead,
and he wears a smile.

What motivates him most

is what he finds deep down inside.

It's a colorful

world that we live in.

A beautiful world that we live in.

CELEBRATE all our differences.

What's in the heart
matters most of all.

It's a colorful world that we live in.

It's a beautiful world that we live in.

We have millions
of children
with possibilities,

from the streets of Nairobi

to the hills of Tennessee.

Every hand you touch

has a print

with a different name.

What makes this world a *better place*

is that we're not the same.

CELEBRATE all our differences.

It's a colorful world,

a beautiful world

that we live in.

Colorful World

Music by Keith Thomas
Lyrics by CeCe Winans, Keith Thomas, and Alvin Love III

(Chorus)
It's a colorful world, it's a beautiful world that we live in
It's a colorful world, it's a beautiful world that we live in
(It's a colorful world)

She wears nose rings with weird things floating through her hair.
She is slightly embarrassed by everyone who stares.
And when she walks away, you might say she's a little wild.
But she could rule the world when she opens up her mouth and smiles.

It's a colorful world that we live in,
A colorful world that we live in.

(Repeat chorus)

Now he's been cheated, mistreated, for the color of his skin.
He is rarely contrary over what should not have been.
Yet he holds his head up instead, and he wears a smile.
What motivates him most is what he finds deep down inside.

It's a colorful world that we live in,
A colorful world that we live in.

Celebrate all our differences
Instead of building these plastic fences.
What's in the heart matters most of all, most of all.

(Repeat chorus)

We have millions of children with possibilities,
From the streets of Nairobi to the hills of Tennessee.
Every hand you touch has a print with a different name.
What makes this world a better place is that we're not the same.

Celebrate all our differences
Instead of building these plastic fences.
What's in the heart matters most of all.
Celebrate all our differences
Instead of building these plastic fences.
What's in the heart matters most of all, most of all.

(Repeat chorus)